Ratio Analysis

:: Author ::

Pareshkumar M. Thakor

PUBLISHED BY

The New Era International Publishing House
HQ. At & Po. Chaveli., Ta- Chansma,
Dist- Patan, North Gujarat, India, Asia.
www.iphouseindia.com

First Publication: 13th April, 2015

Copyright: Author

(c) **Pareshkumar M. Thakor**

ISBN:- 978-15-12121-87-2

Price: Rs.750/- INDIA
        $ 15 OUTSIDE INDIA

PUBLISHED BY

**The New Era International Publishing House
HQ. At & Po. Chaveli., Ta- Chansma,
Dist- Patan, North Gujarat, India, Asia.
www.iphouseindia.com**

What is Ratio Analysis ?

Ratio analysis is one of the oldest methods of financial statements analysis. It was developed by banks and other lenders to help them chose amongst competing companies asking for their credit. Two sets of financial statements can be difficult to compare. The effect of time, of being in different industries and having different styles of conducting business can make it almost impossible to come up with a conclusion as to which company is a better investment. Ratio analysis helps creditors solve these issues. Here is how:

What are Financial Ratios ?

- **Shortcut:** Financial ratios provide a sort of heuristic or thumb rule that investors can apply to understand the true financial position of a company. There are recommended values that specific ratios must fall within. Whereas in other cases, the values for comparison are derived from other companies or the same companies own previous records. However, instead of undertaking a complete tedious analysis, financial ratios helps investors shortlist companies that meet their criteria.

- **Sneak-Peek:** Investors have limited data to make their decisions with. They do not know what the state of affairs of the company truly is. The financial statements provide the window for them to look at the internal operations of the company. Financial ratios make financial analysis simpler. They also help investors compare the relationships between various income statement and balance sheet items, providing them with a sneak peek of what truly is happening behind the scenes in the company.

- **Connecting the Dots:** Over the years investors have realized that financial ratios have incredible power in revealing the true state of affairs of a company. Analyses like the DuPont Analysis have brought to the forefront the inter-relationship between ratios and how they help a company become more profitable.

Sources of Data

Here is where the investors get the data they require for ratio analysis:

- **Financial Statements:** The financial data published by the company and its competitors is the prime source of information for ratio analysis.

- **Best Practices Reports:** There are a wide range of consulting firms that collate and publish data about various companies. This data is used for operational benchmarking and can also be used for financial data analysis.

- **Market:** The data generated by all the activity on the stock exchange is also important from ratio analysis point of view. There is a whole class of ratios where the stock price is compared with earnings, cash flow and such other metrics to check if it is fairly priced.

Techniques Used in Ratio Analysis

Ratio, as the name suggests, is nothing more than one number divided by the other. However, they become useful when they are put in some sort of context. This means that when an analysts looks at the number resulting out of a ratio calculation he/she must have a reasonable basis to compare it with. Only when the analyst looks at the number and compares it what the ideal state of affairs should be like, do the numbers become powerful tool of management and financial analysis.

Dividing numbers and obtaining ratios is therefore not the main skill. In fact this part can be automated and done by the computer. Companies wouldn't want to pay analysts for doing simple division, would they?. **The real skill lies in being able to interpret these numbers**. Here are some common techniques used in the interpretation of these numbers.

Horizontal Analysis

Horizontal analysis is an industry jargon for comparison of the same ratio over time. Once a ratio is calculated, it is compared with what the value was in the previous quarter, the previous years, or many years in case the analyst is trying to make a trend. This provides more information of two grounds. They are:

- Horizontal analysis clarifies whether the company has a stable track record or is the value of the ratio influenced by one time special circumstances.

- Horizontal analysis helps to unveil trends which help analysts unveil trends in the performance of the business. This helps them make more accurate future projections and value the share correctly.

Cross-Sectional Analysis

Cross sectional ratio analysis is the industry jargon used to denote comparison of ratios with other companies. The other companies may or may not belong to the same industry. Cross sectional analysis helps an analyst understand how well a company is performing relative to its peers. In a way this removes the effect of business cycles. There are many variations of cross sectional analysis. They are as follows:

- **Industry Average:** The most popular method is to take the industry average and compare it with the ratios of the firm. This provides a measure of how the company is performing in comparison to an average firm.

- **Industry Leader:** Many companies and analysts are not satisfied with being average. They want to be the industry leader and therefore benchmark against them.

- **Best Practice:** In case, the company is the industrial leader, then it usually crosses the industry border and seeks inspiration from anyone anywhere in the world. They benchmark with the best practices across the globe.

Importance of Different Ratios to Different User Groups

As we have seen earlier that there is a wide variety of financial ratios available. They fall into many categories and if variations are included there are hundreds of types of ratios that are common in practice. However, all the ratios are not used by everyone on a regular basis. There are some ratios which are more important to some user groups than they are to other user groups. This is explains why this is the case:

Management: Turnover and Operating Performance Ratios

The management of the company may not be so concerned with the results. They are usually more interested in the cause. This is because while other classes of stakeholders do not have control over the working of the firm i.e. the cause, the management does. All the other stakeholders question the management at the annual general meeting. Hence, management tries to get as much insight into the ratios as possible. They create operating performance ratios and compare it to their previous performance and to the performance of others to learn from the past as well as to be able to give satisfactory answers to the investors.

Shareholders: Profitability

Shareholders, for obvious reasons, are most concerned about profitability. Their investments are at risk and they expect to gain the maximum. Investors scrutinize profitability numbers and pounce upon the slightest signs of mismanagement. For the shareholders, the profitability ratios are the beginning point. They then follow the trail the ratios leave. However over the past two decades the focus has been steadily shifting towards cash flow ratios.

Debt holders and Suppliers: Cash Flow and Liquidity

Debt holders and suppliers are concerned whether they will be paid the amount promised to them at the date that was promised to them. It is for this reason that they are very concerned about the liquidity of the firm. Slightest signs of liquidity issues are met with supply cutbacks from suppliers. The fact that debt holders are concerned about the same ratios creates a self reinforcing negative loop for the company. This is because at the same time when suppliers cut credit and supplies, debt holders refuse to lend more money and the whole situation becomes a cash crunch.

Credit Rating Agencies: Solvency

While debt holders are suppliers are concerned about short term liquidity and cash flow, credit rating agencies go a step ahead. They use solvency ratios to rigorously analyze whether the company will be able to make good its obligations in the long run.

Limitations of Ratio Analysis

Ratio analysis, without a doubt, is amongst the most powerful tools of financial analysis. Any investor, who wants to be more efficient at their job, must devote more time towards understanding ratios and ratio analysis. However, this does not mean that it is free of limitations. **Like all techniques, financial ratios have their limitations too. Understanding the limitations will help investors understand the possible shortcomings with ratios and avoid them**. Here are the shortcomings:

Misleading Financial Statements

The first and foremost threat to ratio analysis is deliberate misleading statements issued by the management. The management of most companies is aware that investors look at certain numbers like sales, earnings, cash flow etc very seriously. Other numbers on the financial statements do not get such attention. They therefore manipulate the numbers within the legal framework to make important metrics look good. This is a common practice amongst publically listed companies and is called "Window Dressing". Investors need to be aware of such window dressing and must be careful in calculating and interpreting ratios based on these numbers.

Incomparability

Comparison is the crux of ratio analysis. Once ratios have been calculated, they need to be compared with other companies or over time. However, many times companies have accounting policies that do not match with each other. This makes it impossible to have any meaningful ratio analysis. Regulators all over the world are striving to make financial statements standardized. However in many cases, companies can still choose accounting policies which will make their statements incomparable.

Qualitative Factors

Comparison over time is another important technique used in ratio analysis. It is called horizontal analysis. However, many times comparison over time is meaningless because of inflation. Two companies may be using the same machine with the same efficiency but one will have a better ratio because it bought the machine earlier at a low price. Also, since the machine was purchased earlier, it may be closer to impairment. But the ratio does not reflect this.

Subjective Interpretation

Financial ratios are established "thumb of rules" about the way a business should operate. However some of these rules of thumb have become obsolete. Therefore when companies come with a new kind of business model, ratios show that the company is not a good investment. In reality the company is just "unconventional". Many may even call these companies innovative. Ratio analysis of such companies does not provide meaningful information. Investors must look further to make their decisions.

Capital Structure Ratios - Meaning and Importance

Capital structure ratios are very important to analyze the financial statements of any company for the following reasons:

- ### Same Business Can Yield Different Returns

Investors understand that the way a business is funded can have a lot of impact on the returns it provides. Although the total return provided will always be the same, the way those returns are distributed amongst investors will vary. It is for this reason that investors pay careful attention to these ratios as they help them understand the consequences of the best and worst possible scenarios.

- ### Combination That Reduces Total Cost of Capital

A firm is a legal entity that has nothing when it first begins operations. It acquires capital in the form of debt and equity on different terms. Debt has fixed returns but sure repayments. Equity on the other hand has uncertain returns but the probability of returns that far exceed those of debt-holders. There is a cost attached to both debt and equity and the purpose of an ideal capital structure is to minimize the total cost.

- **Nature of Capital Employed Can Magnify Returns**

The specific combination of debt and equity employed is capable of magnifying returns (both gains and losses) for equity investors. Therefore they have a special interest in ensuring that the capital structure and leverage position of the firm is in control.

- **Solvency of the Firm**

An incorrect capital structure can mean ruin of an otherwise healthy firm. This is because, if the firm is funded by too much debt, it has a lot of interest bills to pay. Therefore in a lean period, the firm is likely to default on its interest obligations. The worst part is that if the firm defaults a few times, debt holders have the right to seek legal counsel and start liquidating the firm. In such a scenario, an otherwise healthy firm may have to sell its assets at throw away prices. Thus an ideal capital structure is one that provides enough cushions to shareholders so that they can leverage the debt-holders funds but it should also provide surety to debt holders of the return of their principal and interest. Since capital structure ratios reveal these facts, analyst pay careful attention to them.

. **Liquidation of the Firm**

Capital structure ratios help investors analyze what would happen to their investments in the worst possible scenario. In case of liquidation senior debt holders have the first claim, then junior debt holders and then in the end equity holders get paid if there is anything left. Investors can gauge what they are likely to recover if the organization went bust immediately.

Debt to Equity Ratio - Meaning, Assumptions and Interpretation

The debt to equity ratio is the most important of all capital adequacy ratios. It is seen by investors and analysts worldwide as the true measure of riskiness of the firm. This ratio is often quoted in the financials of the company as well as in discussions pertaining to the financial health of the company in TV shows newspapers etc.

Formula

Debt to Equity Ratio = Total Debt / Total Equity

The total equity includes retained earnings which have been listed on the balance sheet

There is subjectivity with regards to treatment of preference shares. Some companies add them to debt while others add them to equity based on the relative features of the preference shares issued. However, usually the quantum of preference shares in not big enough to make a difference.

Meaning

The debt to equity ratio tells the shareholders as well as debt holders the relative amounts they are contributing to the capital. It needs to be understood that it is a part to part comparison and not a part to whole comparison.

Assumptions

The debt to equity ratio measures the amount of debt based on the figures stated in the balance sheet. Of late there have been many ways figured out to take on debt without it showing up on the balance sheet. The debt to equity ratio is a very old measure and is not meant to take into account such complication. Some analysts factor in off balance sheet debt as well to get a better picture. However, they do not have enough information to be very accurate at this endeavor.

Interpretation

Debt to equity ratio provides two very important pieces of information to the analysts. They have been listed below.

- **Interest Expenses:** A high debt to equity ratio implies a high interest expense. Along with the interest expense the company also has to redeem some of the debt it issued in the past which is due for maturity. This means a huge expense. Moreover this expense needs to be paid in cash, which has the potential to hurt the cash flow of the firm. Investors are never keen on investing in cash strapped firm and therefore have a keen eye on this ratio.

- **Liquidation Scenario:** Another interpretation of the debt equity ratio is the event of a liquidation of the company. Shareholders as well as debt holders want to know what the maximum downside is and debt to equity ratio helps them understand what they would end up with if the company were to stop functioning as a going concern.

Debt Ratio - Formula, Meaning, Assumptions and Interpretation

The debt ratio is the second most important ratio when it comes to gauging the capital structure and solvency an organization. This is provides an in-depth look.

Formula

Debt Ratio = Total Debt / Total Capital

The debt ratio is a part to whole comparison as compared to debt to equity ratio which is a part to part comparison. Another major difference between the debt to equity ratio and the debt ratio is the fact that debt to equity ratio uses only long term debt while debt ratio uses total debt.

Total debt means current liabilities are also included in the calculation and so is the debt due for maturity in the coming year.

Meaning

The debt ratio tells the investment community the amount of funds that have been contributed by creditors instead of the shareholders. The creditors of the firm accept a lower rate of return for fixed secure payments whereas shareholders prefer the uncertainty and risk for higher payments. If too much capital of the company is being contributed by the creditors it means that debt holders are taking on all of the risk and they start demanding higher rates of interest to compensate them for the same.

Assumptions

Like debt to equity ratio, the debt ratio assumes the absence of off balance sheet financing. However given the fact that companies now indulge in structured finance and derivatives to a very large extent this assumption seems unreasonable.

Interpretation

The debt ratio of a company is highly subjective. There is no such thing as an ideal debt ratio. Neither are industry wide comparisons very helpful because the capital structure of a company is an internal decision. Here is how to interpret the debt ratio of a company.

- **Certainty:** Debt is not harmful as long as the revenues in question are fairly certain. Debt becomes a problem when the revenues of the company are wildly fluctuating. This is when there arise situations when the company may not have enough cash on hand to meet its interest obligations. Hence while looking at the debt ratio analysts usually also look at the revenues with regards to how certain they are to gauge the riskiness. Whether these revenues are converted to cash fast enough to meet the interest obligations is also under consideration.

- **Tax Shield Advantages:** Debt is a tax deductible expense. Hence the amount of interest paid reduces the tax bill of the company. One of the advantages of having a higher debt ratio is that you have to pay less to the government in taxes.

Equity to Fixed Assets Ratio

Formula

Equity to Fixed Assets Ratio = Equity / Total Fixed Assets

- Equity includes the retained earnings
- Total Fixed assets excludes intangible assets of the firm

Meaning

The "equity to fixed assets" ratio shows analysts the relative exposure of shareholders and debt holders to the fixed assets of the firm. Thus, if the "equity to fixed assets" ratio is 0.9, this means that shareholders have financed 90% of the fixed assets of the company. The remaining 10% as well as current assets and investments have all been financed by debt holders.

Assumptions

There is an implicit assumption that the number of shares outstanding has remained unchanged. This is because the ratio measures the total amount of equity. The total amount of equity can be increased by issuing shares at lower prices to the public or to the promoters. However, this may not be a desirable scenario since more shares means a loss to individual shareholders.

Interpretation

The "equity to fixed assets" ratio is used by a variety of stakeholders for different purposes. The common interpretations that are drawn based on this ratio have been listed below:

- **Creditworthiness:** Bankers and other lenders use the "equity to fixed assets" ratio widely. They use it to understand how much of the fixed assets of the firm are already financed by debt. A firm with a low "equity to fixed assets" ratio has not utilized its credit to the maximum and therefore extension of credit is relatively secure. This is because in the event of a liquidation, the creditors have the first claim over the proceeds recovered from the assets.

- **Conservative vs. Aggressive:** What might be good news for the bankers may not be such great news for the equity shareholders. This is because if the firm has a very low "fixed assets to equity" ratio, it means that the firm is underutilizing its credit. This means that the shareholders could have achieved a higher rate of return in case the company managed its operations better and used credit to its advantage. Hence a high "equity to fixed assets" ratio is not a very good sign either.

- **Less than 0.65 Not Recommended:** Based on empirical evidence, certain analysts have concluded that companies that have a "equity to fixed assets" ratio of less than 0.65 are very risky bets. Companies where shareholders own less than 65% of the fixed assets are likely to cash strapped and debt ridden. These companies usually run into solvency and liquidity issues and therefore must be avoided.

Proprietary Ratio - Meaning, Assumptions and its Interpretation

The proprietary ratio is not amongst the commonly used ratios. Very few analysts prescribe its usage. This is because in reality it is the inverse of debt ratio. A higher debt ratio would imply a lower proprietary ratio and vice versa. Hence this ratio does not reveal any new information.

Formula

Proprietary Ratio = Total Equity / Debt + Equity

Meaning

The proprietary ratio is the inverse of debt ratio. It is a part to whole comparison. The proprietary ratio measures the amount of funds that investors have contributed towards the capital of a firm in relation to the total capital that is required by the firm to conduct operations.

Assumptions

- **No off Balance Sheet Debt:** The presence of off balance sheet debt may understate the total debt that the firm has. This in turn will overstate the proprietary ratio. Such accounting can be thought of as deceptive because it masks the true risk profile of the business. However, since accountants would be on the right side of the rules, it is not incorrect for them to do so.

Interpretation

- **Depends on Risk Appetite:** The ideal value of the proprietary ratio of the company depends on the risk appetite of the investors. If the investors agree to take a large amount of risk, then a lower proprietary ratio is preferred. This is because, more debt means more leverage means profits and losses both will be magnified. The result will be highly uncertain payoffs for the investors.

On the other hand, if investors are from the old school of thought, they would prefer to keep the proprietary ratio high. This ensures less leverage and more stable returns to the shareholders.

- **Depends on Stage of Growth:** The ideal value of the proprietary ratio also depends upon the stage of growth the company is in. Most companies require a lot of capital when they are at the early stages. Issuing too much equity could dilute the earnings potential at this stage. Therefore a lower proprietary ratio would be desirable at such a stage allowing the firm to access the capital it wants at a lower cost.

- **Depends on Nature of Business:** The firm has to undertake many risks and balance them out. There are market risks which are external to the firm and there are capital structure risks that are internal to the firm. If the external risks are high, the firm must not undertake aggressive financing because this could lead to a complete washout of the firm. On the other hand, if the external environment is stable, the firm can afford to take more risks.

Interest Coverage Ratio - Meaning, Assumptions and Interpretation

The interest coverage ratio is a number that has a lot of importance for the creditors of the firm. This number tells them how safe their investments are and how likely they are to get back principal and interest on time.

Formula

Interest Coverage Ratio = EBIT / Interest

Meaning

The interest coverage ratio tells investors how many rupees they have made in profit, per rupee of interest that they owe to their shareholders. Thus if the interest coverage ratio is 3, then the firm has 3 rupees in profit for every 1 rupee in interest obligations. Thus profits will have to fall by more than 66% for the firm to register a loss.

Assumption

The standard assumption of no accounting manipulation in either of the two numbers involved (EBIT and Interest expenses in this case) is made while calculating the interest coverage ratio.

Interpretation

- **Higher Ratio Means Solvent:** The higher the interest coverage ratio of any firm, the more solvent it is. If an organization, under normal circumstances, earns way more than what its interest costs are, then it is financially secure. This is because earnings would have to take a real beating for the firm to default on its obligations. Hence, interest coverage ratio is of prime importance to lenders like banks and bond traders. Credit rating agencies also pay close attention to this number before they rate the company.

- **Tolerance Depends On Variability:** In industries where sales are very stable, such as utilities companies, a lower interest coverage ratio should suffice. This is because, these industries, by nature record stable revenues. Hence the sales and profits of the company are unlikely to witness wild fluctuation. This means that even in tough times the company will most probably be able to make good its interest obligations because its performance is not affected by the business cycle.

On the other hand, companies with highly variable sales, like technology and apparel companies, need to have a high interest coverage ratio. These industries are prone to wild fluctuations is sales and investors want to ensure that their cash flow is not interrupted as a result. Hence they demand a higher interest coverage ratio before they give out their money.

- **Ability To Take On More Credit:** This is a corollary of the fact that high interest coverage ratio means the company is solvent. Lenders want to lend money to people who are solvent. This ensures that they get repaid on time and the risks of business are assumed by the owner. Thus, companies with high interest coverage ratios are more likely to get credit easily and on more favorable terms.

Degree of Financial Leverage Ratio

A high debt equity ratio makes the company financed by debt more than by equity. Therefore there are fixed interest payments involved. Hence when the going is good, the company makes a handsome return as a small percentage of change in EBIT creates a large percentage change in earnings per share. However the inverse of this is also true. Just like financial leverage helps to magnify profits, it also magnifies losses when EBIT fall down. Analysts want to quantify exactly how much variability does debt funding create in the operations of a particular company and have created a measure called "Degree of Financial Leverage" which we will study in detail.

Formula

Degree of Financial Leverage = % Change in EPS / % Change in EPS

There is a reasonable assumption about the absence of any changes in accounting policy which would make the EPS and EBIT figures incomparable from the previous years.

Example

- **Profit Magnification Example:** The best example of degree of financial leverage is in the field of home ownership. Let's say that you brought a house for Rs 100. It is financed 30% by own money and 70% by debt bearing interest of 10%.

Thus, you are obligated to pay Rs 7 interest each year, regardless of what happens. Lets say that the price of the house went up by 20% to 120. In this case you will pay back the creditors Rs 77 (principal + interest) and be left with Rs 43. Since your original investment was Rs 30, you have gained Rs 13.

A price increase of 20% has led to an increase in the shareholders return by approximately 43%!

- **Loss Magnification Example:** Let's say that you brought the same house for Rs 100. It is financed 30% by own money and 70% by debt bearing interest of 10%.

Thus, you are obligated to pay Rs 7 interest each year, regardless of what happens. Lets say that the price of the house went down by 20% to Rs 80. In this case you will pay back the creditors Rs 77 (principal + interest) and be left with Rs 3. Since your original investment was Rs 30, you have lost Rs 27.

A price decrease of 20% has led to a decrease in the shareholders return by approximately 90%

Interpretation

Leverage is very dangerous unless the company is reasonably certain of its earnings. Investors view the leverage ratio with great detail. This is because it enables a small change in the EBIT to completely wipe out the company's capital and make it insolvent almost overnight.

Degree of Operating Leverage Ratio

The degree of operating leverage of a company is very important from an investor's standpoint. Although it shows the riskiness of a venture, it also shows the efficiency of a company. Just like, financial leverage arises out of the capital structure of a company, operating leverage arises out of its cost structure. If a company has too many expenses which are fixed in nature, the company is said to have high operating leverage.

Typically companies that are highly mechanized have high operating leverage. This is because they have replaced labor which is a variable cost by depreciation on machinery which is a fixed cost. This creates debate whether having a high operating leverage is a bad thing. Henry Ford was amongst the first to use operational leverage on a large scale and build cars at a fraction of what it would cost earlier. This idea was soon followed by many others and high operating leverage became the norm.

Formula

Degree of Financial Leverage = % Change in Sales / % Change In EBIT

The ratio makes a reasonable assumption that accounting policies have not changed so much that the Sales and EBIT figures do not remain comparable across companies or across time.

Example

- **Profit Magnification Example:** In case a company has a high operating leverage, most of its costs are fixed. Consider for example, the movie business. The costs incurred to make the movie are fixed. Hence when tickets are sold, the first few tickets go towards recovery of the cost of production. However, once a breakeven point has been reached, entirely all the money goes towards the bottom line. Hence a slight change in sales has the capability to magnify and bring about a big change in EBIT.

- **Loss Magnification Example:** However, every lever has its flipside and operating leverage is no exception. Since most of the costs are fixed, in the vent of a downturn, the company does not have the opportunity to cut costs. In many cases, companies are not able to fulfill their requirements to meet the fixed cost obligation. Whereas all companies are hurt in the event of a downturn, companies with excessively high operating leverage are wiped out in such events.

Interpretation

Whether operating leverage is good or bad for a company depends on the nature of its operations and stability of its cash flow streams. In case of stable operations, high operational leverage in desirable and even recommended.

Degree of Combined Leverage Ratio

Most firms use both operating leverage and capital leverage to some extent. In today's business world it is almost impossible to run a business without having some degree of automation and mechanization (operating leverage). It is also not possible to grow at an adequate speed unless the company is taking advantage of borrowed money.

However, the degree to which a company uses operating leverage and financial leverage can be different. Some companies use more financial leverage than operating leverage while other use more operating leverage. This creates a challenging scenario whereas an analyst has to interpret the different degrees of riskiness of companies with different cost and capital structures. The degree of combined leverage (DCL) makes it possible to do this.

Formula

- **Degree of Combined Leverage = %Change in EPS / %Change in Sales**

- **Degree of Combined Leverage = Degree of Operating Leverage * Degree of Financial Leverage**

Example

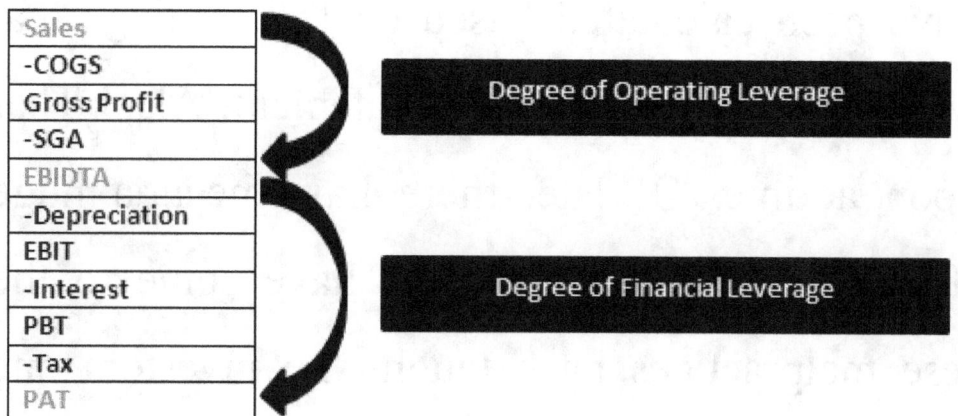

PAT / Number of Shares = Earnings per Share (EPS)

Therefore if operating leverage of a firm= 1.4 whereas financial leverage = 2, then the degree of combined leverage equals 1.4*2 = 2.8

Interpretation

Degree of operating leverage shows how a change in sales affects the EBIDTA of the firm. Whereas degree of financial leverage shows how a change in EBIDTA affects the EPS of the firm. Combining the two analysts can predict how a change in sales is likely to magnify the gains or losses to the EPS.

Introduction to Cash Flow Ratios

Once upon a time, investors and analysts used to believe in ratios that have been calculated based on the earnings that the company has stated in the Income Statement. Alas! That was once upon a time. Of late, there have been a huge number of frauds and malpractices that have come to the fore. All these malpractices have taught the investors one lesson only. The lesson is that fact that corporate income statements and balance sheets are susceptible to fraud. This is because the numbers in these statements are based on the policies that management sets. Thus, in the seas of fraud, they have found truth in cash flow ratios. Here is why cash flow ratios are so important and form the backbone of any financial analysis conducted today.

Cash Flow is Fact

Cash flow is fact, all else is error, or at least susceptible to error. The company cannot fudge how much cash it has in the bank. The auditors are supposed to confirm with the bank the amount of cash that they have in the company's accounts and verify the same with what the company has stated. How the company received this cash is also made clear by the cash flow statement. Hence, it is the least susceptible to fraud and provides the truest picture of the state of affairs.

Company Expenses Cash

The company cannot pay its employees in earnings. Neither can it pay its creditors or suppliers in earnings. The fact of the matter is that the company needs cash like humans need oxygen to stay alive. A few days without adequate cash and the company may not survive. This is the reason investors want to ensure that they have enough cash on hand to meet forthcoming obligations. To many investors it seems insane that expenses like interest be compared with earnings since if earnings are not converted to cash, they cannot pay expenses. Therefore cash is what matters!

Company Invests Cash

The company invests cash when it makes capital expenditures. These capital expenditures are what makes the company's profits and cash flow grow in the future. Therefore, it makes more sense to consider cash flow rather than earnings while trying to gauge the rate at which the company will grow in the future.

There is no Consensus on Definition of Cash Flow

There is a slight problem with cash flow ratios though. There has been no consensus on what constitutes cash flow. Hence there are many measures of cash flow instead of one. This leads to there being multiple ratios.

Cash Flow to Debt Ratio

Formula

Cash Flow to Debt Ratio = Operating Cash Flow / Total Debt

Meaning

The cash flow to debt ratio tells investors how much cash flow the company generated from its regular operating activities compared to the total debt it has. For instance if the ratio is 0.25, then the operating cash flow was one fourth of the total debt the company has on its books. This debt includes interest payments, principal payments and even lease payments to cover off balance sheet financing.

Assumptions

- **Does Not Cover Amortization:** The cash flow to debt ratio assumes interest and principle payments will be paid in the same manner over the years as they have been paid in this year. This assumption is implicit in the fact that while calculating total debt (denominator) we take the interest and principal payments from the present year financial statements.

However, this may not be the case. Companies have access to a variety of financing schemes. Some of these schemes include interest only payments, bullet payments, balloon payments, negative amortization, so on and so forth. In such innovative amortization, there may be years when the company has to pay a lot of interest and other years when it has to pay none. Hence the present years figures may not be indicative of the future.

- **Does Not Cover Lease Increment:** Once again, the ratio takes the lease numbers from the financial statements of the current year. However, most lease contracts nowadays have lease increment provisions in them. This means that every year the lease may go up by a certain percentage. The ratio does not cover this aspect.

Interpretation

- **Creditworthiness:** Cash flow to debt ratio is the true measure of the creditworthiness of a firm. This is because a company has to pay its interest and retire its debt by paying cash. They cannot pass on the earnings that they may have recorded on accrual basis to creditors to satisfy their claims. Earlier analysis used earnings because at that time credit periods were small or nonexistent and therefore earnings to some extent meant cash flow. However, with the proliferation of credit, the distinction has been widened. A company may book earnings immediately and not receive cash for years on end. Thus creditors have their eyes set on cash flow ratios.

- **Analysis of the Past:** The cash flow to debt ratio thus becomes an analysis of how comfortably the company paid its obligations in the past. The future may or may not be similar. Analysts have to make adjustments to this ratio to make it more meaningful.

Free Cash Flow to Operating Cash Flow Ratio

The free cash flow to operating cash flow ratio is different from other ratios. It is different in the sense that it is comparing two measures of cash flow. Usually cash flow ratios compare a cash flow item to an item on the income statement or on the balance sheet. Here are the details of this ratio:

Defining the Terms

The terms used in the ratio i.e. operating cash flow as well as free cash flow have been described in the cash flow section. But here is a quick refresher.

Operating Cash Flow: Operating cash flow is considered by many to be the most appropriate measure of cash flow. It measures the cash flow that the company has been able to generate from its regular day to day operations. Cash flow generated from onetime events such as sale of assets and investments is not a part of this. Hence investors can expect this cash flow to continue in the next period.

Free Cash Flow: Free cash flow is not listed on the cash flow statement. Rather it is derived by subtracting the capital expenditure from operating cash flow. This measure is important because this is the amount of cash flow that the investors have left after meeting the growth needs of the firm.

Formula

The name of the ratio pretty much gives away the formula. The formula is as follows:

Free Cash Flow to Operating Cash Flow Ratio = Free Cash Flow / Operating Cash Flow

Meaning

This ratio tells the investors about how much free cash flow is being generated for every rupee of operating cash flow. A higher ratio means company is not investing too much in capital expenditure and therefore maybe a mature company that is not seeking any more growth but rather seeking to sustain its operations.

Interpretation

- **Compare With Maturity of the Firm:** The stage of maturity of the firm has a huge impact on the free cash flow to operating cash flow ratio. Mature stable firms do not need to make too many capital investments and thus have a higher ratio. On the other hand companies that are growing will have a lower ratio. One needs to start questioning if mature companies have lower ratios or vice versa.

. **Gestation Period:** The gestation period is the time that is taken for the capital expenditure to start producing revenues and cash flows. A company with a high gestation period will invest more and more each year, the effects of which will not be visible in the free cash flow to operating cash flow ratio until many years.

Operating Cash Flow to Sales Ratio

Formula

The formula for this ratio can be easily judged by its name:

Operating Cash Flow to Sales Ratio = Operating Cash Flow / Sales

Meaning

. **Used Over a Period of Time:** Conclusions must not be drawn based on a single number. A company may be able to convert its sales to cash for one year. But it is consistent, sustained record to do so that makes it more valuable.

. **Cash Flow Should Move In Direction And Proportion With Sales:** If the sales are genuine, the cash flow will move more or less in correlation with the sales figure. The direction of movement and the quantum of change must be highly correlated with the sales figures.

Assumptions

• **Earnings Have Not Been Manipulated:** As has been discussed many times before, earnings are subject to easy manipulation by the management. Thus if the management changes the policies from one year to another, then the numbers are just not comparable.

• **Cash Flow Has Not Been Manipulated:** The total cash flow cannot be manipulated. However, companies have got innovative and have indeed shifted cash flow from financing and investing sections to the operating section. Thus analysts need to be wary of such accounting tricks at play to make the numbers look better than they are.

Interpretation

• **Are The Company's Sales Genuine:** The operating cash flow to sales ratio provides the analyst insight into the sales of the company. It is a known fact that companies can fudge the sales number relatively easily. This can be done by changing the revenue recognition policy which allows accountants to book future income as income today. Sometimes companies do fake transactions to ensure that sales numbers look good to the stock market. However, the acid test comes when sales need to be converted to cash. Only genuine sales bring in cash flow. Thus analysts can make more accurate prediction of the future years cash flows and therefore value the stock more accurately.

- **Compare With Days Sales Outstanding:** The operating cash flow to sales ratio should also be somewhat in line with the days receivables outstanding ratio. For instance if 90 days receivables are outstanding, it means on an average the company extends credit for (90/360), 25% of its sales at any given point of time. Thus in this case the operating cash flow to sales ratio must be 75% or close. This makes the analysts more sure that the financial statements of the firm are indeed genuine.

Market Related Ratios - Meaning and Its Importance

Most investors do not invest directly in the company i.e. they are not promoters of the company. Rather they invest in the company through the stock market. This means that they buy shares at a certain value and make a profit only when the price of the shares go up or they get regular dividends from their investments or a combination of both. This is the reason why investors are particularly interested in how the current share price of the company compares with its fundamentals. Market related ratios help investors use the numbers stated on the balance sheet to better their understanding of the same.

What Are Market Related Ratios?

Market related ratios compare the current stock price of the company which is being quoted on the stock exchange to various balance sheet, income statement and cash flow items. One component of all market related ratios is the current stock price.

Why the Stock Price Is Not the Actual Price?

It is important to understand that the quoted stock price is not the actual price of the share. The stock price just means the price that you are paying to obtain a fraction of the earnings of the company. So if you are buying 1 share at USD 10 and there are 100 shares, you own 1% of the company. This 1% ownership means you get 1% of the profit, which in our case is let's say USD 2. Hence the actual price you are paying is USD 10 to buy a future recurring profit stream of USD 2 per share. Of course these profits subject to risks and that is what makes investing challenging.

Since the quoted stock price is not the actual price, market related ratios offer a window to analysts using which they can gauge whether a stock is over or under valued and then act accordingly.

How Do These Ratios Help In Valuation?

- **Expose the Fundamentals:** Unless the market is being completely driven by sentiments at a given point of time, market related ratios expose the fundamentals of the company in question. This is because prices in the stock market are generally a reflection of the long term value that investors see in the company.

- **Makes It Easier to Maintain Changes in the Stock Price:** Investors can compare changes in fundamentals to changes in stock prices to see whether or not the share is fairly valued. Market related ratios have been long used by savvy investors to make successful long term investments.

Price to Earnings (PE) Ratio

The price to earnings ratio is the most fundamental of all market related ratios. It has been used for decades by stalwarts in the investment community. However, it is also the ratio that has come under maximum fire from the skeptics. A variety of measurements have been developed to compensate for what skeptics call the lack of correct information provided by the price earnings ratio. Almost all other market related ratios are a variation of the price to earnings ratio.

Formula

Price to Earnings Ratio = Current Market Price / Reported Earnings of the Company

Meaning

The price to earnings ratio tells the investors how many rupees they are paying for every rupee in earnings that the company presently has. If the price to earnings ratio is 5, then investors are paying 5 rupees to get a stream of earnings of 1 rupee per year till perpetuity. This ratio therefore also implicitly tells the payback period which in this case would be 5 years.

Assumptions

There are a lot of assumptions that the price to earnings ratio implicitly makes. This is the reason that this ratio has come under a lot of criticisms from skeptics who think that price to earnings ratio provides a distorted image of what the reality of the company really is. The common assumptions are as follows:

- **Earnings are Stable:** The price to earnings ratio implicitly assumes that the earnings of a given company will remain stable over the period of time that the investment made is being recovered. However, this is seldom the case. Businesses are subject to business cycles and earnings move cyclically. The world is yet to see a company that has been able to generate stable earnings for an extended period of time. This is why the price earnings ratio may present reality to be different than what it really is.

- **Earnings Have Not Been Manipulated:** There is a lot of evidence that the earnings of a company are subject to gross manipulation. The management has an unfair control over what it can project to the investment community as earnings. Moreover the investment community may not enough data at hand to adjust these earnings and arrive at a figure which they think are fair earnings of the company. Hence, naïve investors who only look at price-earnings ratios without looking at whether the earnings have been manipulated will possibly make wrong decisions based on this number.

Interpretation

The price to earnings ratio must be interpreted in the light of the fundamentals of finance. These fundamentals are the fact that an investment grows over a period of time. This growth pattern usually follows an exponential pattern which makes the phenomenon of compounding so important.

- Does Not Factor In Growth Rates
- Does Not Factor In Compounding

The fact that price to earnings ratio uses simple arithmetic division makes it unacceptable to many skeptics in the investment community.

Price Earnings Growth (PEG) Ratio

The Price Earnings Growth (PEG) Ratio is one of the first variations that were made to the Price to Earnings Ratio to make it more meaningful. The full form of the PEG Ratio is Price Earnings Growth ratio. Instead of being a two way comparison between price and earnings, the PEG ratio makes a three way comparison. The first step is to arrive at the price to earnings ratio whereas the next step is to divide this ratio by the growth rate of the company to arrive at the PEG ratio.

The PEG ratio was developed because investors argued that current stock market price is an expectation of future gains to be made by the company in question. Therefore valuing it solely on the basis of the current year's earnings is incorrect. They realized that two companies could currently have the same earnings but the one that has been growing its earnings faster needs a better valuation. It is for this reason that they started factoring in growth rates before concluding whether the company is fairly prices.

Formula

PEG Ratio = Price to Earnings Ratio / Growth Rate

The growth rate is calculated based on historic data. Analysts could use as much data as they feel is comfortable without losing the current trend of earnings of the company in question. This growth rate is usually expected as a percentage out of 100. For example, if a company has a growth rate of 20% and a P/E Ratio of 30. Then the PEG Ratio will be:

PEG Ratio = 30/20 = 1.5

Assumptions

- **Growth Rate Expected to Continue:** The PEG Ratio is an extension on the P/E Ratio and therefore makes some of the audacious assumptions that the P/E Ratio makes as well. The PEG Ratio assumes that the current rate of growth of the company is expected to continue. However, in reality trends usually last for 4 to 5 years. So by the time the analyst does figure out the trend, it would be affected by the cyclical nature of business and may have changed.

Interpretation

- **Fairly Priced Will Equal Growth Rate:** Veteran investors place a lot of faith in the PEG ratio. They believe that in the long term, the P/E ratio of the company will always equal its growth rate. Therefore if the PEG ratio is equal to 1, then the company is fairly priced. This means that investors must actively scout for companies with PEG ratios less than 1.

Price to Book Value Ratio

Formula

Price to Book Value = Current Market Price / Total Assets – Intangible Assets

The value of assets is taken from the most recently published balance sheet.

Meaning

The price to book value ratio looks at an immediate liquidation scenario. Investors therefore compare the price that they are paying for the company against what they would receive if the business shut operations right away.

Assumptions

- **Intangible Assets are Worthless:** The price to book value excludes intangible assets from the calculation of book value. This can be misleading since intangible assets like patents can provide cash flows even if the company is being liquidated immediately.

- **Tangible Assets are Represented at Fair Price:** The ratio assumes that management have stated the assets at their fair book value i.e. there has been no manipulation using less depreciation to make the assets look overvalued.

Interpretation

The price to book value ratio can be used to make some serious interpretations about the business of the company and how the market is reacting to it. Here are some of the common interpretations made on the basis of price to book value ratio:

- **Underpriced or Fundamentally Wrong:** A lower price to book value ratio is a very rare occurrence. All companies that are traded on the stock exchange are usually valued above what they have in assets. However, when such a scenario arises, one of the two situations is true. Either the market has overlooked a possible free lunch or the market knows that there are some serious flaws in the fundamental nature of the business. The analyst must therefore look at a low price to book value ratio as a starting point to understand which of the two is the reality.

- **Bankruptcy Bets:** The price to book value has proved to be very useful for speculators making bankruptcy bets. A useful example of this would be the Satyam fiasco. When it was discovered that there was a fraud of huge magnitude in the company, everyone wanted to get rid of the share. In this mania, the stock price plummeted to an unrealistically low level. Investors who had an eye on the Price to Book Value ratio found that even if the company wound up its operations at its book value, they would still be left with more book value per share than the then prevailing market price per share. Such bets are usually risky because it is difficult to trust the book value stated on financials that have been admitted to be doctored with.

Price to Cash Flow Ratio

"Cash is King" say the bigwigs on Wall Street. That is why the valuation of shares is done on the basis of discounted cash flow model rather than discounted earnings model. The price to cash flow ratio provides an analyst with a shortcut for finding companies that have been undervalued in comparison to their cash flows. Analysts can scan through the price to cash flow ratios of a number of companies. Then they can start paying more attention to the companies where these values seem to be abnormally low. This is describes price to cash flow ratio is more detail.

Formula

There are many different measures of what analysts consider to be the true cash flow of the company. Some analysts consider operating cash flow i.e. cash flow generated from regular activities to be the correct measure. Others think that the capital investments that the company needs to make must be separated and the resultant free cash flow provides a better picture of the company's fundamentals. Accordingly there are at least two cash flow measures that an analyst can look at and here are their formulas:

Price to Operating Cash Flow = Current Market Price / Operating Cash Flow

Price to Free Cash Flow = Current Market Price / Free Cash Flow

Meaning

The price to cash flow ratio tells the investor the number of rupees that they are paying for every rupee in cash flow that the company earns. Thus if the price to cash flow ratio is 3, then the investors are paying 3 rupees for a stream of future cash flows of 1 rupee each. This cash flow is passed on to the investors as dividend. In case, it is reinvested in the business, it shows up as capital appreciation. Thus cash flow will help the investors gain in one way or another.

Interpretation

- **Cannot be Manipulated:** The price to cash flow ratio is considered to be a more stringent measure by many. The basic reason being that cash flow cannot be manipulated. Cash in the bank is a fact unlike earnings which are the management's opinion. Charges like depreciation, changes in inventory and revenue policy do not affect the cash position making it the favorite of skeptics.

- **No Effect of Compounding:** The price to cash flow ratio does not consider the effect of compounding. Once cash is received it can be immediately put to work to earn even more cash. However, the ratio fails to capture this phenomenon.

Price to Sales Ratio

Formula

Price to Sales Ratio = Current Market Price / Reported Sales Revenue

Many companies state their revenue after removing the effects of onetime events whereas others continue to state the revenue without any adjustments.

Meaning

The price to sales ratio tells an investor how many dollars they are paying for every dollar that the company has in sales. Hence if the price to sales ratio is 3, investors are paying 3 dollars for every dollar in sales. This needs to be benchmarked against the industry average to understand the context.

Assumptions

As in all market value ratios, there is an unrealistic assumption in price to sales ratio too. The assumption is that sales will continue to behave in the same manner for an extended period of time. However, analysts are not so concerned about sales being absolutely flat for an extended period of time. They are more concerned about the average value of sales for the future periods being the same or higher than it currently is.

Interpretation

- **More Sales Mean More Profits:** Investors often assume that the company will make more sales and earn the same rate of return that it is currently earning. However, this assumption is against the fundamental laws of economics. Economics state that price must be reduced to achieve a higher sales volume. It also stated that costs decrease when scale increases. Hence the profitability of the company is unlikely to be the same with increasing or decreasing sales volumes.

- **More Reliable Than Earnings:** Proponents of the price to sales ratio are mostly critics of the price to earnings ratio. They understand the importance of comparing the current market price to fundamentals in the financials of the firm. However, they believe earnings are subject to too much manipulation which can be difficult to detect. Sales on the other hand are subject to less manipulation. The sales figure can only be manipulated if there is a change in the revenue recognition policy. This policy is one of the first that is read by analysts and any manipulation here is easily detected.

- **Sales Are Subject To Manipulation Too:** There have been cases where sales have been wrongly stated without corresponding changes in the revenue recognition policy. However, these are cases of outright fraud rather than cooking the books. There is very little an investor can do to protect against such frauds.

As an absolute measure, price to sales ratio may not be perfect. However, ration analysis is not about absolute perfection. Price to sales is a better indicator of the fundamentals of the company as compared to price to book value, in the opinion of many critics.

Dividend Yield Ratio

Investors can be classified into types. The two predominant types are growth oriented investors and value oriented investors. Growth oriented investors invest in young growing companies. They expect returns in the form of capital appreciation backed by the high rate growth in the operations and profitability of the firm. On the other hand value investors invest in mature stable companies and expect returns in the form of stable cash flows paid in the form on dividends over and over again. The Dividend Yield ratio is meant for the second type of investors i.e. the value investors.

Formula

Dividend Yield = Annualized Dividend / Current Stock Price

Most companies pay dividends on a quarterly basis rather than on an annual basis. Hence for the purpose of finding out the dividend yield, analysts often annualize the dividend paid in the most recent quarter. They think it better projects the dividend paying ability of a company.

Meaning

Value investors often look at the stock of a company, the way a real estate investor looks at rental properties. They expect to put money one down one time and expect to receive payments for the rest of their lives. Hence the dividend yield tells them a percentage of their original investment that they would receive each year, if they invested in the stocks right away.

Assumptions

The dividend yield ratio assumes that the company in question will continue making dividend payments at the same or higher rate than it is currently doing. A historical analysis of the stock market will validate this assumption. Historically companies that have been making dividend payments continue to do so. This is because a dividend cut is adversely received by the market as a very negative signal and the share price immediately plummets. It is therefore reasonable to assume that the company will continue to pay dividends until something untoward happens.

Interpretation

The dividend yield company must be compared to competing investment options to get a better picture of the operations of the firm. It must also be applied to the company's own historical records to validate the fact that it has indeed been making regular dividend payments.

- **Stable Mature Companies:** Dividend yield ratio is meaningful only when it is applied to stable mature companies. Companies in the field of utilities, hotels etc which have a regular and dependable cash flow are the ones in which dividend payout ratio is an important metric.

- **Often Negligible:** In advanced economy companies like IT, Electronics and communication, the dividend payout ratio is negligible. Investors look at these companies as engines of growth and not as avenues of stable cash flow.

Put Call Ratio - Formula, Meaning, Variations and Interpretation

The put call ratio is the only financial ratio that does not compare the current market price to any financial statement item. Rather it compares what investors plan to do with a given stock or an index at a later date. Put and call are derivative options. The put option gives the seller a right but not an obligation to sell, however the call option gives the buyer a right but not the obligation to buy. Analyzing the put call ratio can give the investors some insight about where the stock is headed for in the near future. This ratio is more relevant to short term price movements rather than long term ones and is hence more widely used by speculators who are looking to make a quick buck.

Formula

Put Call Ratio = Number of Put Options / Number of Call Options

This data is periodically published by the exchange. Hence investors can easily have a look at these numbers.

Meaning

A high put call ratio signals a bearish trend in the future and indicates that short selling must be done to profit from this change. On the other hand, a low put call ratio indicates a bullish trend which speculators perceive as a signal to go long.

Variations

Many speculators believe that the put call ratio does not represent the true picture. This is why there are a few variations of the put call ratio that are used. Before making a call based on any put call ratio, investors must understand what variation is being used and therefore how to interpret it. Common variations are as follows:

Moving Average: Instead of using the put call data for a single day, speculators usually use data for an extended period of time. Usually the moving average used is that of 21 days. However, the number of days can be different.

Money Weighted: Some speculators feel that money weighted put call ratio is a better indicator since it informs about the possible number of options that will be exercised.

Interpretation

Billionaire investors like George Soros are known to have used the put call ratio to predict the market sentiment. It is said that investors who have a constant eye on the put call ratio can gauge changes in market sentiment faster than other investors and have a lead time in modifying their positions and thereby benefitting from the change.

Introduction to Liquidity Ratios

Liquidity can be defined as the ability of a firm to make good its short term obligations. Most businesses function on credit. Hence to run a business firms have to both extend credit as well as ensure that they receive credit as well. Liquidity ratios measure the relationship between the amounts of short term capital that the firm has locked in its receivables versus the short term interest free debt it has acquired in the form of accounts payables.

Liquidity ratios can be defined as the ratios which help analysts predict the short term solvency of the firm. Short term here is meant to be considered the period until the next business cycle which is usually 12 months.

Liquidity is the Life of a Business

A firm seldom has all the resources it needs to run the business. It gets credit from its employees, suppliers, customers, the government and such other entities. Each of these entities extends credit to the firm on the assumption that it will make good its obligations when they are due. Such obligations are usually due in the short term. Investors are therefore very cautious about ascertaining whether the firm does in fact have the capability to meet these obligations. Liquidity ratios help in ascertaining this. With secondary data that is available in the annual reports of the company, analysts often make projections about whether the company has enough resources to survive the short run without hampering its reputation or operations.

Liquidity has an Impact on Long Term Survival of the Firm

Amateur investors think liquidity is primarily short term. It does not matter whether or not the company can pay its immediate bills, if the long term prospects of the company look good, it is a good investment. This is the farthest from the truth as history has shown liquidity issues can have far reaching effects on the health of a firm sometimes even endangering the very survival of the firm. Here is how it happens:

- Banks Ask For Higher Interest Payments
- Suppliers Are Wary Of Extending Credit
- Attracting And Retaining Best Employees May Be As Issue

As a result of all these, present profitability is compromised and so are the future growth plans of the company which now has to seek funds at extremely high costs.

The best example of how liquidity problems can wreak havoc and threaten the very survival of a firm is the recent Kingfisher Airlines fiasco where the firm had to shut down operations because it could not meet its short term obligations.

Current Ratio - Formula, Meaning, Assumptions and Interpretations

The current ratio is the most popularly used metric to gauge the short term solvency of a company. This is provides the details about this ratio.

Formula

Current Ratio = Current Assets / Current Liabilities

Meaning

Current ratio measures the current assets of the company in comparison to its current liabilities. This means that the firm expects to collect cash from the people that owe it money and pay to the ones that they owe money to on time. Hence if the current ratio is 1.2:1, then for every 1 dollar that the firm owes its creditors, it is owed 1.2 by its debtors.

The ideal current ratio is 2 meaning that for every 1 dollar in current liabilities, the company must have 2 in current assets. However, this varies widely based on the industry in which the company is functioning.

Assumptions

The current ratio makes two very important assumptions. They are as follows:

- The current ratio assumes that the inventory that the company has on hand will be liquidated at the price at which it is present on the balance sheet. However, this may not be the case. Many times inventories become obsolete and have to either be discarded on sold off at a fraction of the cost that they were purchased for. The current ratio does not warn the investors about these risks.

- The current ratio assumes that the debtors of the firm will pay it on time. There is nothing wrong with this belief if it is founded based on strong facts. The analyst must look at the past performance of the firm in collecting its receivables and factor in the late payments and bad debt charges to make the calculation more meaningful.

Wrong Interpretations

- A moderately high current ratio is considered safe and healthy. However, if the current ratio is too high, it means that company is not effectively managing its current assets. Common symptoms include a lot of obsolete inventory as well as trouble getting paid on time by the debtors.

- A current ratio shows the company's liabilities and assets position for the next 12 months. It is possible that the liabilities may be due in the next 6 months whereas the assets may be due for realization only after 9 months. The current ratio does not provide conclusive information about the liquidity position of the company.

- Since receivables are included in the calculation, an analyst must also be aware about the age of these receivables. Older receivables are less likely to be collected and therefore investors must be careful about making predictions based on these receivables.

Quick Ratio - Meaning, Formula and Assumptions

The quick ratio is a variation of the current ratio. However, a quick ratio is considered by many to be a more conservative estimate than the current ratio. This characteristic fetches it the nickname of being the "Acid test ratio".

The difference between the current ratio and the quick ratio is the fact that quick ratio excludes the inventory. In theory this may seem like a small difference, however in practice anyone who is aware about the difficulties involved in liquidating inventories at the right price will vouch for the conservativeness of this ratio. The quick ratio has been discussed in greater detail in this is.

Formula

Quick Ratio = (Current Assets - Inventories) / Current Liabilities

Meaning

The quick ratio checks the company's performance to fulfill its obligations in a situation when it is not able to liquidate its inventory. In such a situation the company will have to pay its current liabilities out of the cash and cash equivalents that it has on hand and the amount of money it has already tied up in accounts receivables. The ideal quick ratio is considered to be 1:1. However, this varies widely according to the different credit cycles prevalent if different industries. Hence an analyst must look at competing firms and the industry average before forming opinions based on the current ratio.

Assumptions

There are no assumptions made regarding the inventory, because it is excluded from the calculation of this ratio. However, there are assumptions made about debtors and the fact that they will pay up on time to finance the payment of short term liabilities that a company has on hand.

Wrong Interpretations

- The quick ratio of the company can become unreasonably higher because of a large amount of accounts receivables that the company may have on hand. The true measure of the liquidity management of a company is its ability to complete the cash to cash cycle in the fastest possible time. However if the company has a track record of being able to recover its dues on time large receivable may be overlooked.

- Since the quick ratio is a variation of the current ratio it suffers from all the shortcomings faced by the current ratio.

Cash Ratio - Meaning, Formula and Assumptions

The cash ratio is limited in its usefulness to investors and financial analysts. It is the least popular of the liquidity ratios and is used only when the company under question is under absolute duress. Only in desperate circumstances do situations arise where the company is not able to meet its short term obligations by liquidating its inventory and receivables and this is when the cash ratio comes handy.

Formula

Cash Ratio = (Cash + Cash Equivalents + Marketable Securities) / Current Liabilities

Meaning

The cash ratio indicates the amount of cash that the company has on hand to meet its current liabilities. A cash ratio of 0.2 would mean that for every rupee the company owes creditors in the next 12 months it has 0.2 in cash. 0.2 is considered to be the ideal cash ratio.

Assumptions

The cash ratio is the most stringent of all liquidity ratios. Hence there are no assumptions made. The cash and cash equivalent figures stated on the balance sheet are facts and so are the current liabilities stated on the balance sheet. Hence there is no assumption about future events that need to occur as per the company's plan.

The nearest the cash ratio gets to an assumption is that it believes that marketable securities and cash equivalents can be quickly liquidated. Under normal circumstances this is always the case. The only case where liquidation of these securities would be an issue would be the complete failure of the economic system.

Wrong Interpretations

- A high cash ratio may not be a good thing for a company. Cash is an idle asset. It does not earn a sufficient rate of return. Therefore companies must constantly work towards keeping the cash locked up in gainfully employed investments. A large amount of cash on the balance sheet may be an indicator that the company is running out of investment opportunities.

- Wild fluctuations in the cash ratio may not be such a bad thing either. It is not uncommon for companies to keep accumulating cash and then using it at one go when a profitable opportunity arises. It is this nature of the cash ratio that makes its usefulness limited. The cash ratio usually creates more questions than it answers for the financial analysts. Given the fact that analyst may not access to inside information to answer these questions, the usefulness of these ratios remain limited.

- Moreover, cash received is not necessarily cash earned. The cash can be in the form of payments received in advance. Moreover, third parties may have the right to demand the payment of that cash. These rights do not appear on the balance sheet in the current liabilities but are present in the footnotes and hence are not used in the calculation of the ratio.

What is Negative Working Capital ?

Traditional financial analysts would consider a negative working capital i.e. having more current liabilities than current assets, a sign of imminent danger. This view was deep rooted in the belief that a company must always have sufficient cash on hands to meet its short term liabilities failing which the credit will dry up and the company will get into a lot of trouble. However, of late negative working capital has actually become a norm in many industries such as retail. There are thriving businesses such as Wal-Mart that have based their entire business strategies around negative working capital. This paradigm shift in the opinion about negative working capital is what makes it an interesting subject to read further about. This is will provide more details.

What the Current Ratio Would Suggest

As per traditional analysis, investors would look at the current ratio of a company with negative working capital with great concern. As the current assets will be less than the current liabilities, this would signal imminent danger to them. The current ratio of such a company would be less than 1. However as we will see it is more than healthy.

What the Reality Is ?

In some businesses like in retail, inventory is taken from the suppliers on sale or return basis. This has become the norm after big ticket retailers such as Wal-Mart pretty much control the shelf space which in turn controls what people buy. Suppliers of Wal-Mart therefore find Wal-Mart in a commanding position and therefore are more than happy to extend liberal trade terms. These terms state that Wal-Mart must make the payment for the purchases in 45 days if they are able to sell the inventory. In case they are not able to sell it, the suppliers will be more than happy to take the goods back.

Wal-Mart while on one hand has negotiated a 45 day credit for itself, sells to customers on cash. Assuming a period of 10-15 days to actually sell the inventory, Wal-Mart still has one full month of interest free cash for itself. They can use this cash for their treasury operations or to fund future growth of their company. In case they fail to sell the goods within 45 days, they just return the inventory or get an extension.

Hence, a **negative working capital scenario has become beneficial for many companies who meet their operating expenses out of interest free credit extended by the suppliers**.

Introduction to Turnover Ratios

Turnover ratios (also known as efficiency ratios) are a very important class of ratios. These ratios are not only used by financial personnel but also by the people in charge of operations. However, we are going to consider these ratios from the point of view of outside investors. This is because judgments have to be made about the efficiency of the firm based on limited information at hand. Here is an elementary introduction to what turnover ratios are and why they are important.

Efficiency Means Business

Over the years, investors have realized one rule and that is "Efficiency means growing business". Any firm which is more efficient than its peers in producing the same goods and services will be more profitable in the short run. This profitability will allow the firm to build a competitive moat around itself and these businesses often become very valuable. This is like an investors dream formula for success. It is for this reason that investors carefully look at the efficiency numbers of newbie firms.

A Look at Efficiency through Financial Statements

Finding out whether the firm is efficient is difficult even for a manager or an employee who has all the information at hand. Investors on the other hand just have the financial statements. They have to use these financial statements as their window into the operations of the firm. This is possible because every activity done by the firm involves costs and therefore leaves a trail on the financial statements. The turnover ratios are the investors' method to connect the dots. They use information which is available in different financial statements. They then aggregate this information together and make meaningful conclusions about the operations of the company.

The Link between Sales, COGS and Turnover

Turnover ratios as the name suggest, are related to sales. The logic is that given a certain amount of assets, how much sales can a company achieve? Therefore turnover ratios are always a comparison between an income statement item i.e. sales and the corresponding balance sheet item. For example if we compare fixed assets to sales, we get fixed asset turnover ratio. On the other hand when we compare accounts receivable to sales we get accounts receivable turnover ratio.

In case of inventory turnover ratio we use the COGS figure listed on the income statement rather than the sales figure. This is because inventory is reported at the cost price.

In conclusion, turnover ratios provide early clues to the efficiency of a firm. This can go a long way in making a successful investment and therefore an investor must learn how to use these ratios to his/her advantage.

Accounts Receivable Turnover Ratio

Accounts receivable are a very important part of the current assets of any business. Like inventory, accounts receivable are considered a necessary evil to do business. Large companies hardly conduct any transactions on cash basis with their wholesalers and distributors. The transactions are largely conducted on credit and therefore lead to the existence of accounts receivable on the balance sheet.

Accounts receivable are a dangerous item. If the firm is taking too long to collect the accounts receivable, it means that the firm is not utilizing its capital in the best possible way. Buyers are using the firms interest free credit and making delayed payments to the firm which has to arrange for working capital at a cost. Also the older accounts receivable become, the less likely they are to be collected. Hence, accounts receivable turnover ratio is a closely watched number.

Formula for Accounts Receivable Turnover Ratio

Accounts Receivable Turnover Ratio = Net Credit Sales / Average Accounts Receivable[*]

Average Accounts Receivables = (Beginning Accounts Receivables + Ending Accounts Receivables) / 2

This formula converted to a percentage shows the average amount of receivables that the firm has at any given point of time. Let's say the answer was 27%, it would mean that on an average the firm has 27% of its receivables outstanding at any given point of time.

Number of Days Outstanding Ratio

The number of days of receivables outstanding is considered by many to be a different ratio when in reality it is just an extension of the same ratio. In the above case we have reached an answer expressed in terms of percentage. All we need to do is to convert the answer to the number of days. Lets use the above example to understand how the number of days is calculated.

Number of Days Receivables Outstanding = (27 / 100) * 360

*For the purpose of calculation of ratios accountants assume that the year has 360 days.

The answer to the above is 97.2 days. The firm therefore turns over its receivables every 97.2 days. This means that the old receivables are replaced by a new set of receivables every 97.2 days. Therefore in 360 days, the receivables are turned over (360/97.2) 3.7 times.

Interpretation

The accounts receivables ratio is a good indicator of the bargaining power that a firm has amongst its buyers. If the firm has good bargaining power, there will be less receivable outstanding and the turnover will be higher.

Accounts Payable Turnover Ratio

Just like accounts receivable turnover ratio show the financing that the firm is providing to its buyers interest free, the accounts payable turnover ratio show the financing that the firm is able to receive from its vendors and suppliers free of cost. Since there are no interest charges involved and this is purely trade credit, the objective of the firm ideally should be to pay its bills as late as possible. By doing so, they are using the vendors money to temporarily finance their own business without any cost attached. However, due care must be taken that vendors are not passing off the finance charges in the form of higher prices for products purchased. In that case, the firm may be better off using its own money to buy products at a lower price from vendors that charge a lower price.

The Formula

Accounts Payable Turnover Ratio = Net Credit Purchase / Average Accounts Payables[*]

Average Accounts Payables = (Beginning Accounts Payables + Ending Accounts Payables) / 2

This formula converted to a percentage shows the average amount of payables that are outstanding. The calculation of this ratio is just like the calculation of accounts receivable turnover ratio. Hence we can use the same example to understand the calculation of this ratio as well. However in this case we shall consider the accounts payables to be 40% of all credit purchases

Number of Days Outstanding Ratio

The calculation of number of days outstanding ratio therefore is as follows:

Number of Days Receivables Outstanding = (40 / 100) * 360

*For the purpose of calculation of ratios accountants assume that the year has 360 days.**

The answer to the above is 144 days. The firm therefore pays its bills every 144 days on an average. This means that the old bills are replaced a new set of bills every 144 days.

Therefore in 360 days, the receivables are turned over (360 / 144) 2.5 times.

Interpretation

The accounts payable turnover ratio can be considered to be the exact inverse of the accounts receivable turnover ratio. In that case the objective was to receive payments as soon as possible. Here the objective is to delay payments as much as possible and utilize this free source of funds to finance the firm's own business short term. Bargaining power once again has a big role to play in the accounts payable ratio. A lower accounts payable ratio entails that the firm has the bargaining power which allows it to pay its vendor late. However, COGS of the company must also be checked to ensure that more payment period is not being passed off as high price to the firm.

Fixed Asset Turnover Ratio

Fixed assets i.e. property, plant and equipment represent the single largest investment any company makes in its operations. It is therefore important that a company keeps a close eye on whether these investments are performing well and generating adequate revenue and profit to justify the expenditure. While it is impossible to come up with a single number that explains the efficiency of the company in utilizing its fixed assets, the fixed asset turnover ratio comes close. Here are the details of this ratio.

The Formula

Fixed Asset Turnover Ratio = Sales Revenue / Total Fixed Assets (Average of the two balance sheets)

How to Apply It?

The fixed asset turnover ratio is best applied when there is adequate context. Dividing the two numbers and getting a third number makes little sense unless you can compare it with something.

The best comparison in with the company's past records itself. If the company has made a new addition to the fixed assets, one can find out the new fixed asset turnover ratio and compare it with the old fixed asset turnover ratio and see if there have been any substantial improvements as a result of the addition. Efforts must be made to ensure that extraneous variables like general condition of the economy et al are nullified to get a true picture of the state of affairs.

Another popular comparison is to benchmark the fixed asset turnover ratio of a company with those of other companies in the same industry. Same industry is important because different industries have different fixed capital requirements. Service oriented companies usually have less fixed capital requirement as compared to heavy manufacturing. Some companies use an average of the other companies in the industry to benchmark their performance against whereas others look at the best in the field and try to compete with them.

Interpretation

The fixed asset turnover ratio provides the best estimate of the operating leverage of the firm. If increases in fixed assets lead to disproportionate increases in sales, then the firm has a high operating leverage. In some ways therefore, a wildly fluctuating fixed asset turnover ratio is a measure of high risk that a company is facing.

Also investors should be wary of changes in the revenue policy. Changes in the revenue policy can affect sales which can make this ratio artificially higher or lower thereby distorting the investors perception of the efficiency of the company.

Inventory Turnover Ratio

A company is said to be more efficient when it keeps the least inventory on hand to make the sales it does. The systems of the company must be so efficient that goods are available for sale as and when required and spend the least amount of time waiting in a warehouse. This is because inventory has many costs associated with it. Until earlier it was known as the necessary evil. Not only is capital locked in inventory creating an opportunity cost, there are other costs involved like warehousing, security, insurance, pilferage and so on.

The idea that inventory should be minimized if not eliminated caught the fancy of management gurus from 1980's onwards. Japanese companies showed how they could produce efficiently at lower costs by implementing Just in Time inventory systems. Many years later, Michael Dell revolutionized the computer industry with his made-to-order business model that enabled him to function with zero inventories and earning almost double the profits that entrenched competitors with deep pockets could manage.

Since inventory is such a make or break item in the financials of a company, there is obviously an interest amongst analysts and investors who want to have a close watch on its performance. Hence, the inventory turnover ratio is amongst their favorites. This is explains the inventory turnover ratio in detail.

The Formula

Inventory Turnover Ratio = Cost Of Goods Sold / Average Inventory[*]

- Average Inventory = (Beginning Inventory + Ending Inventory) / 2

- Note that instead of Sales, Cost of Goods Sold is used to calculate this specific turnover ratio. This is because inventories are stored at cost price.

How to Apply it ?

Like all ratios, inventory turnover ratio also needs the same context for the numbers to become meaningful. It needs to be compared with the performance of others. Usually the comparison is done between:

- The company's own inventory turnover ratio for previous years.

- The inventory turnover ratio of other companies in the same or different industry. Different industries are usually considered in the calculation of inventory turnover ratio. This is because the best practices can usually be applied regardless of the industry. Dell's made to order business model has been replicated countless times in different industries.

Interpretation

Caution must be exercised by the analysts in drawing conclusions based on the inventory turnover ratio. Sometimes companies buy large amounts of inventories to beat the forthcoming price hikes. This may show up as an increasing inventory turnover ratio but may not be a bad signal in reality.

Also analysts must be wary of change in inventory policies before calculating and interpreting this ratio.

Working Capital to Sales Ratio - Meaning, Formula, Assumptions and Interpretation

Formula

Working Capital to Sales Ratio = Working Capital / Sales

Meaning

Stating the working capital as an absolute figure makes little sense. Consider two companies, both having the same working capital of USD 100. While one company uses this working capital to generate sales of USD 500, the other uses the same amount as working capital to generate USD 1000 in sales. Which one do you think will be more profitable? Which one do you think is more efficient?

When companies use the same working capital to generate more sales, it means that they are using the same funds over and over again. This is why this ratio is also called "Working Capital Turnover Ratio" as it measures the number of times working capital has been turned over. The higher the sales, the more the profits and therefore the more appropriate use of working capital has been made.

Assumptions

The working capital to sales ratio uses the working capital and sales figures from the previous year's financial statements. Hence, there is obviously an assumption that working capital and sales have been accurately stated. Companies may over stock or under stock because of expectations of shortage of raw materials. These influences are however short term. Thus while reading this number the analyst must compare it with the past numbers to see if this is usual state of affairs for the company or whether this is an exception.

Interpretation

- **Efficiency Vs Riskiness:** While many investors feel that a company must use as little working capital as possible, there are many that have other opinions too. These are conservative investors that fear having too little working capital can be dangerous as it is capable of causing a cash crunch and bringing the operations to a halt. These investors believe that in a cash crunch situation, the company may have to borrow at unfavorable terms nullifying the advantage gained by maintaining lower working capital and causing loss in the form of lost reputation.

These investors may be true because the stock market takes any news of cash shortage very seriously and the stock plummets in the market. But the price in the stock may be short term.

- **Room For Improvement:** Working capital to sales ratio may be a hint to the company that it needs to rethink its policies. If the competitors can get a better deal from suppliers and buyers then the company needs to build more bargaining power in the market. This is a signal that improvements need to be done.

Introduction to Profitability Ratios

The ultimate aim of all business is to generate profit. That is what the investors invest for, management plans for and employees execute for.

Profitability Needs Context

Two companies may be generating the exact same amount of rupee profits, however that does not mean that they are equally profitable. This is because profit is an output measure. And jumping to a conclusion only by looking at the output and not the input that was used to generate the output would not be very prudent! The profit numbers are therefore seen in relation to various measures of inputs like capital, equity, assets etc. Each of these measures tell a separate story about how the company is performing specific to the input. Analysts often use these numbers together, connect the dots and find out the true picture of the company's profitability.

Different User Groups Have Different Needs

Shareholders want the business to generate as much profit as possible. Debt holders on the other hand are content with enough money to ensure that they get paid. Banks want to know whether the company has been making efficient use of fixed assets before granting a loan to buy another one. Thus different user groups have different needs. Hence there is a need for a wide variety of profitability ratios that serves them.

Drivers of Profitability

A careful analysis of the profitability ratios also unearths the drivers of profitability. Analysts can look at the financial ratios of an extended period of time and use correlation analysis to unearth the same. The ability to express the company's business as an accurate input output model is vital for analysts. This is because they can then guess the input, obtain the output and value the firm based on this information. Common drivers of profitability include economies of scale, economies of scope, mechanization, automation, investment in brand value etc.

Cycles and Trends

Industries have their specific business cycles. These business cycles have similar duration and the highs and lows that the business will experience can also be gauged fairly accurately. Profitability ratios help in doing the same. Analysts use many years ratios and then conduct a trend analysis to find out the patterns hidden in the data. This helps them find out how the sales are expected to move in the next quarter.

What are Common Size Statements ?

Common size statements are not financial ratios. Rather they are a way of presenting financial statements that makes them more suitable for analysis. However, analysts always use them in conjunction with ratio analysis. In fact, financial analysts use common size statements as the starting point to help them dig deeper. Common size statements tell them what particular group of ratios deserves more attention for any given set of financial statements.

What Are Common Size Statements ?

Common size statements are financial statements expressed in percentage form. Therefore a common size income statement would consider the sales figure as 100%. Every expense in the income statement will then be expressed as a percentage of the sales figure. Similarly in common size balance sheet the total assets figure is considered to be 100%. Everything else is expressed as a percentage of the same.

Standardized for Comparison

The logic behind creating common size financial statements is that they are easily comparable. Analysts can compare the COGS across two companies and state which one has lower COGS without any calculation! Thus, using the common size statements the analysts look step by step at the financial statements and compare them with other companies. This helps them understand how the company has a different asset structure and cost structure in comparison to its competitors and whether it is favorable or unfavorable for the organization.

Trend Analysis

Trend analysis is analysis which entails comparison with the company's own past performance. The problem in conducting this analysis is that all the numbers keep changing and there is no fixed base. With the help of common size statements, the base gets fixed at 100% and all the numbers can be compared across years. Thus with the help of this trend analysis, a company can figure out whether its advertising costs have gone up compared to last year and if so why?

Sample of a typical common size income statement:

Sales	**100%**

Less: COGS	38%
Gross Profit	62%
Less: SG&A	14%
EBIDTA	48%
Less: Depreciation	10%
EBIT	38%
Less Interest	6%
PBT	32%
Less: Taxes	11%
PAT	21

What are Profit Margins ?

The untrained investor uses profit and profit margin interchangeably. This is not technically correct. The difference may be minor but it is vital. This will explain about profit margins in detail.

Profit vs. Profit Margins

Profit and profitability are two different things. Although they may be closely related, they have a subtle difference. **Profit is the absolute number that a company is earning. Profitability on the other hand implies profit margins**. Margins are calculated on a per unit basis. Secondly they consider the amount of capital that has been employed to generate the profit. Thus profitability i.e. profit margins are a wider concept.

There are different measures of profitability that a company can choose from. Similarly there are different profit margins that a company can choose from. It is common practice to convert each profit figure into a margin.

Based On Competitors

Margins need to be compared with industry and relevant competition. A 15% return may be great for a utility company but may suggest serious problems with an information technology firm. Luxury brands such as Armani, Rolls Royce, and Rolex have very high profit margins. This is because the cost that they put in is small and they are reaping the benefits of the brand that they have created. Comparing a Rolls Royce profit margin to a Maruti would not be advisable even though both of them are cars.

Diminishing Returns Analysis

Profit margins are very important to understand how diminishing returns work in the context of the firm. Using various profit margins, the firm can look at the profitability figures and find out the level of production where the costs are minimum and profit margins are high. This is the quantity that the company should optimally produce.

Cost-Volume Profit Analysis

The drawback with profit margins is that they do not consider volume. It is for this reason that a separate Cost-Volume-Profit analysis often needs to be done. Usually profit margins and volume are inversely proportional to each other. Higher margins indicate lower volumes and vice versa. There are unusual cases where margins and volumes are both high. However, these are usually examples of monopoly.

Return on Assets (ROA) - Meaning, Formula, Assumptions and Interpretation

Another metric that is widely used by investors to gauge the profitability of a company is Return on Assets (ROA). More about this very important ratio has been stated in this.

Formula

Return on Assets = Earnings / Asset Base

. Some calculations may include intangible assets while some others may exclude them from calculation of Return on Assets.

Meaning

The Return on Assets (ROA) ratio shows the relationship between earnings and asset base of the company. The higher the ratio, the better it is. This is because a higher ratio would indicate that the company can produce relatively higher earnings in comparison to its asset base i.e. more capital efficiency.

Assumptions

- ### No Write-downs:

The ROA ratio assumes that the assets have been valued fairly on the books. However, in real life, it is a known fact that companies keep over and/or under valuing their assets to reduce taxation. This may affect the ROA adversely and reduce its usability as a profitability metric.

- ### Excess Cash and Assets for Sale:

The Return on Assets ratio assumes that the company is using all its assets to run the day to day operations. This assumption is likely to be proved incorrect. A lot of companies hold significant cash on their balance sheet. The most valuable company in the world Apple Inc is one such example. Also many other companies hold a lot of impaired and obsolete assets which they plan to sell in the near future. This brings down the Return On Assets (ROA) ratio.

Interpretation

- ### Does Not Depend on Leverage:

Return on assets compares the earnings that a company has generated to its asset base. The asset base could be financed by equity or by debt but it will not make a difference. Return on Assets is therefore independent of leverage.

- **Stage of Growth:**

Return on Assets is very sensitive to the stage of growth that a company is currently experiencing. In the introduction and growth stage, companies invest a lot of money to create asset bases. They may not use the asset base immediately and the benefits may be realized years later. Hence, two companies in the same industry, but at different stages of growth, will have very different Return On Assets.

Return on Invested Capital (ROIC)

Return on Invested Capital (ROIC) is another popular metric that is used widely in financial analysis. The reason for its popularity is that like ROA, ROIC can be used by both equity and debt holders. Also, like ROA, it provides data about return to the company as a whole and is not affected by leverage. Here is more about Return on Invested Capital;

Formula

The formula for calculating ROIC is as follows:

Return on Invested Capital = EBIT / Invested Capital

- **Deriving Invested Capital:** Note that Invested Capital is not the same as Capital listed on the balance sheet. Neither is it the balance sheet total. Invested Capital is a term analysts have coined in the recent past to denote capital that has been listed for the long term in the company's operations. Invested capital is derived by starting from the Balance Sheet Liabilities total and then subtracting the current liabilities from it. This is because current liabilities are not sustainable sources of long term financing and therefore cannot qualify as capital.

Meaning

The Return on Invested Capital (ROIC) metric measures the company's efficiency at allocating its resources to generate the maximum return. Thus ROIC shows the relationship between invested capital and return. It must be thought about as having Rs X in earnings for every rupee in invested capital.

Assumptions

- **Tax Planning not Considered:** The Return on Invested Capital (ROIC) used EBIT which is a pre-tax figure. This ratio does not consider that companies can make significant differences to their profitability with the help of tax planning strategies. Some analysts use both pre-tax and post-tax ROIC numbers to get a better picture of the company's operations.

- **Accurate Book Values:** The Return on Invested Capital (ROIC) assumes that the book values stated are accurate. In many cases, the book values and the market values of assets are very different. One such example is land. Thus, ROIC becomes a misleading figure. This is because many times analysts consider the opportunity cost based on market value and the ROIC drops drastically.

Interpretation

No Break-Up Provided: ROIC does not provide break up about whether income has been earned from regular operations or from one time activities.

Used to Evaluate Acquisitions: Return on Invested Capital (ROIC) is useful in case of companies that have done many acquisitions. Since it is difficult to segregate the cash flows of the two merged companies, ROIC with and without the acquisition serves as a measure of gauging success.